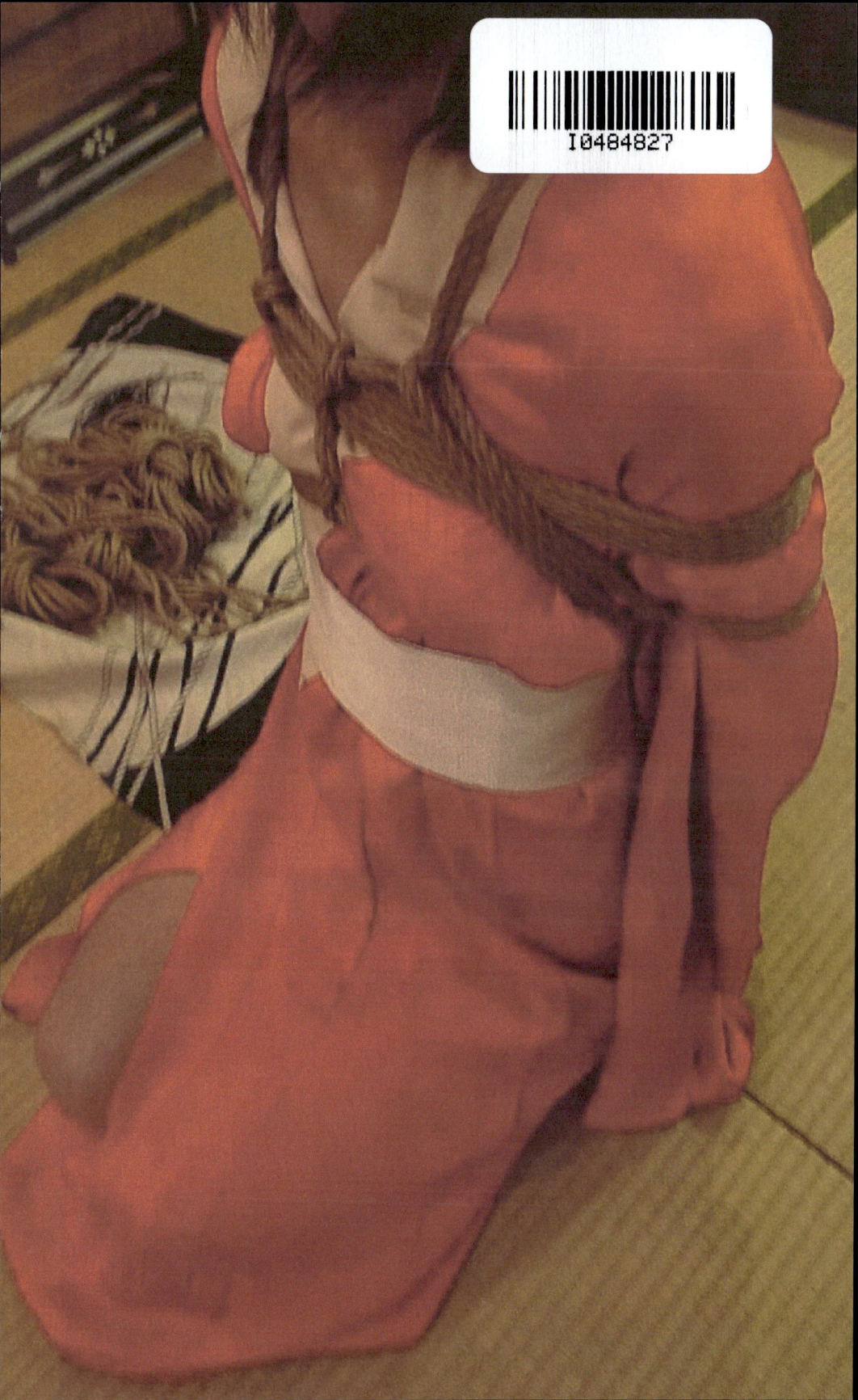

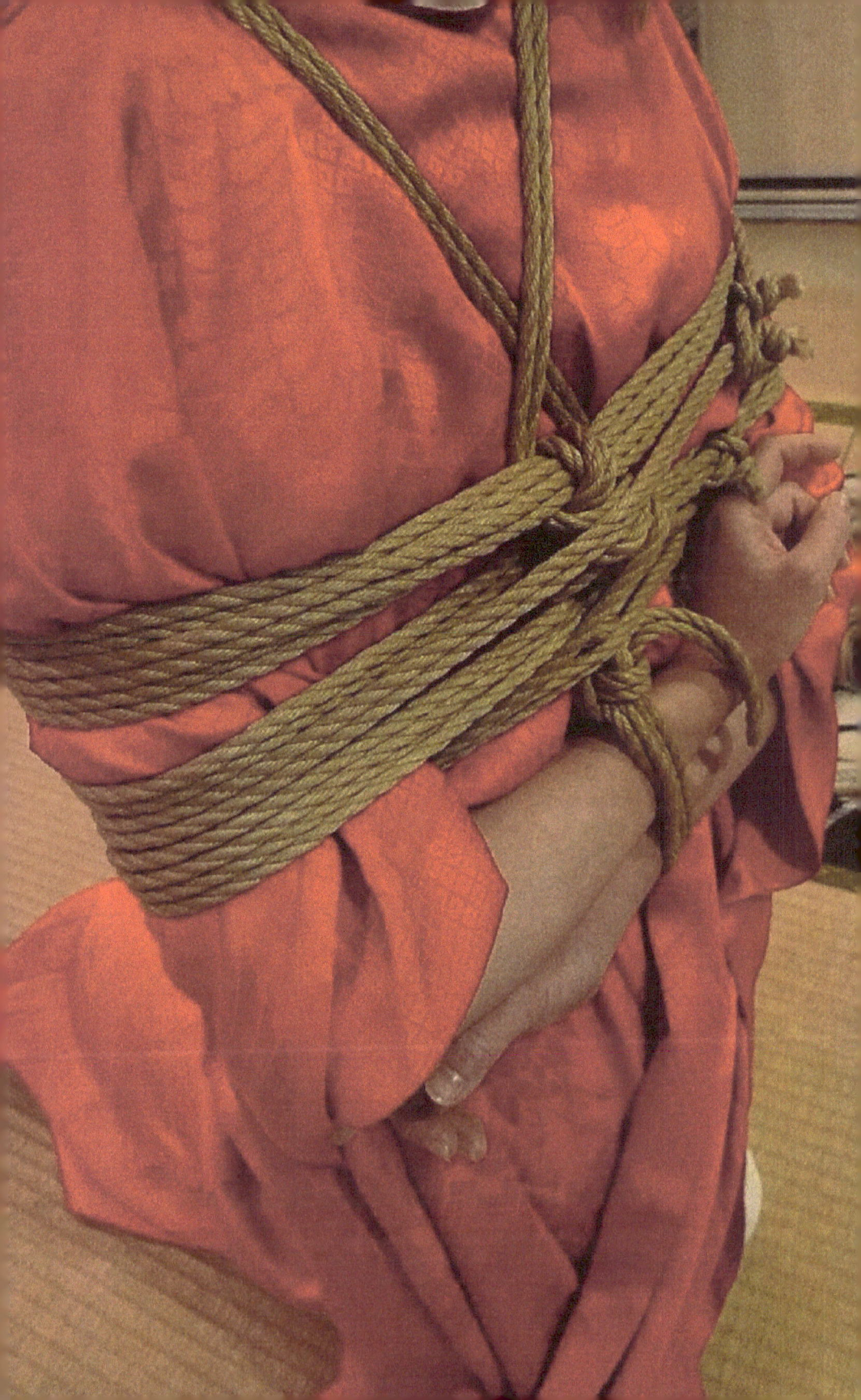

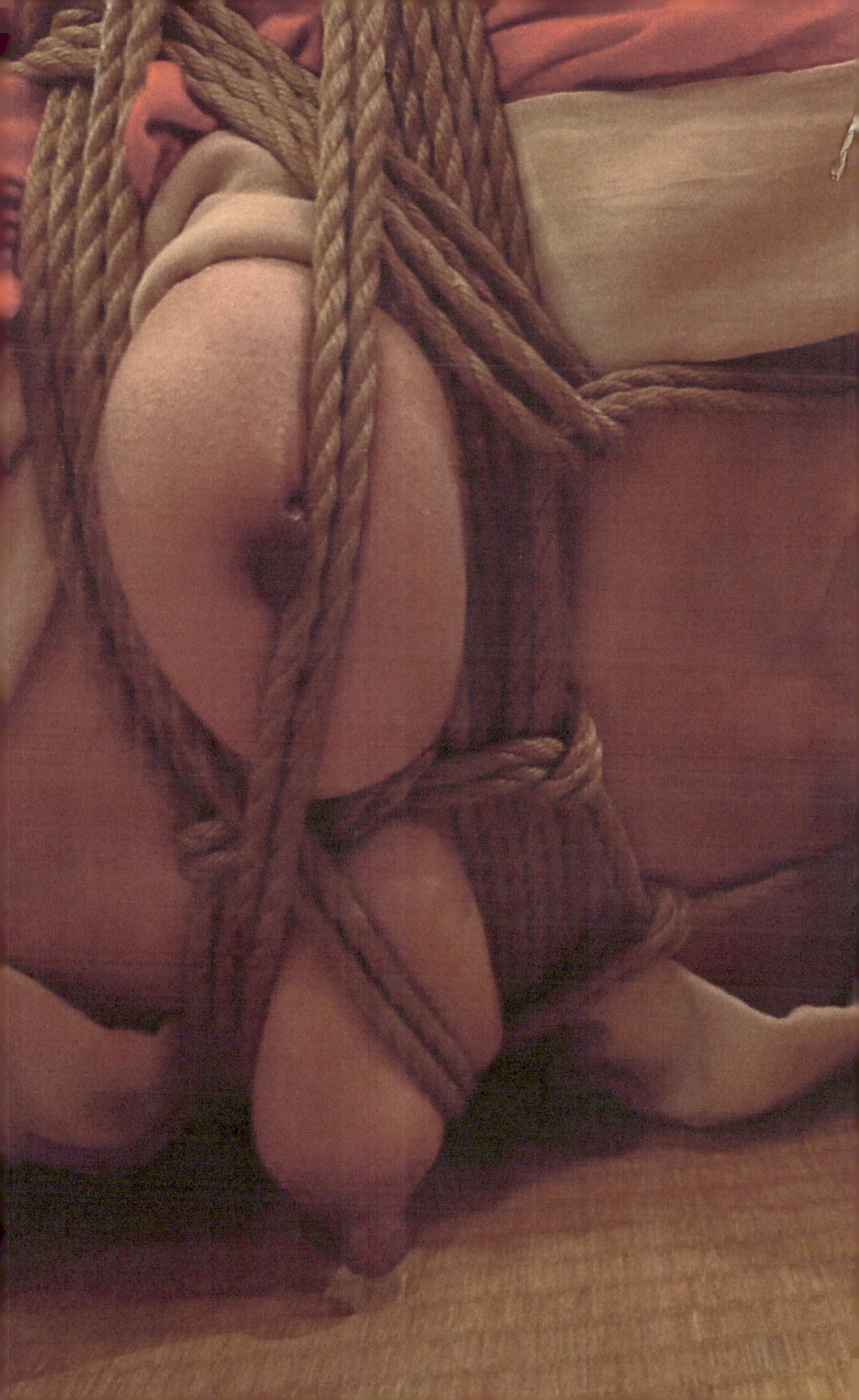

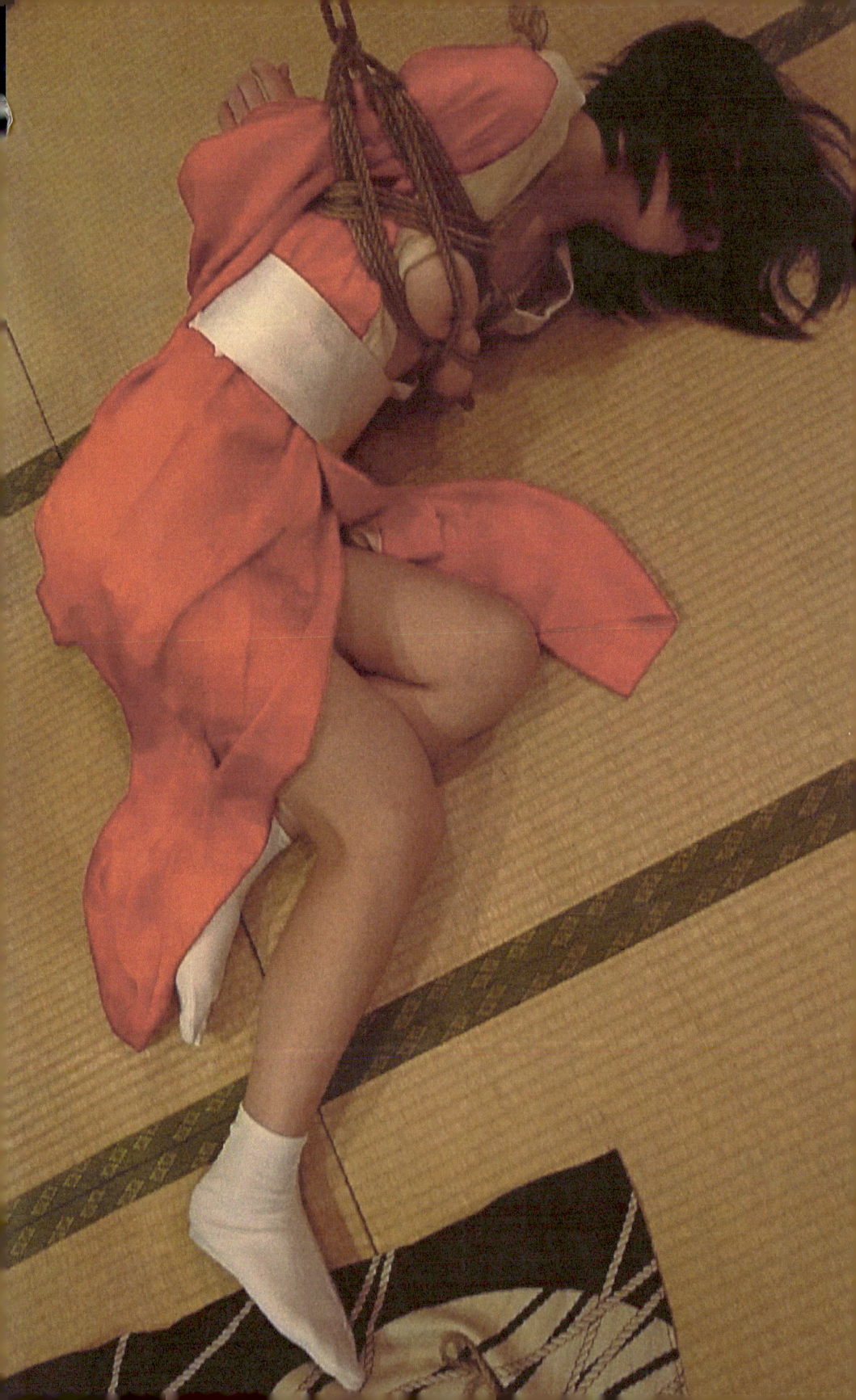

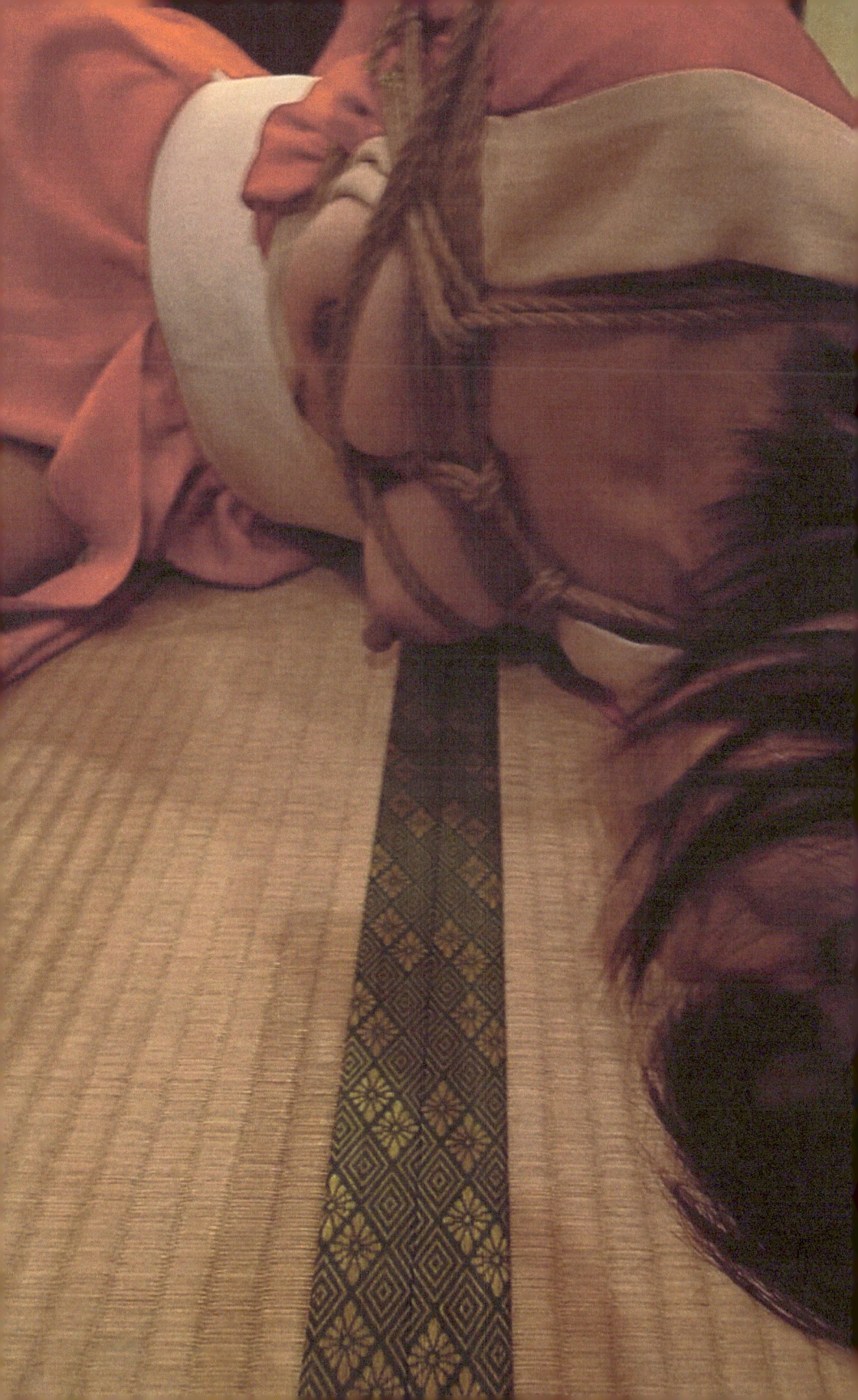

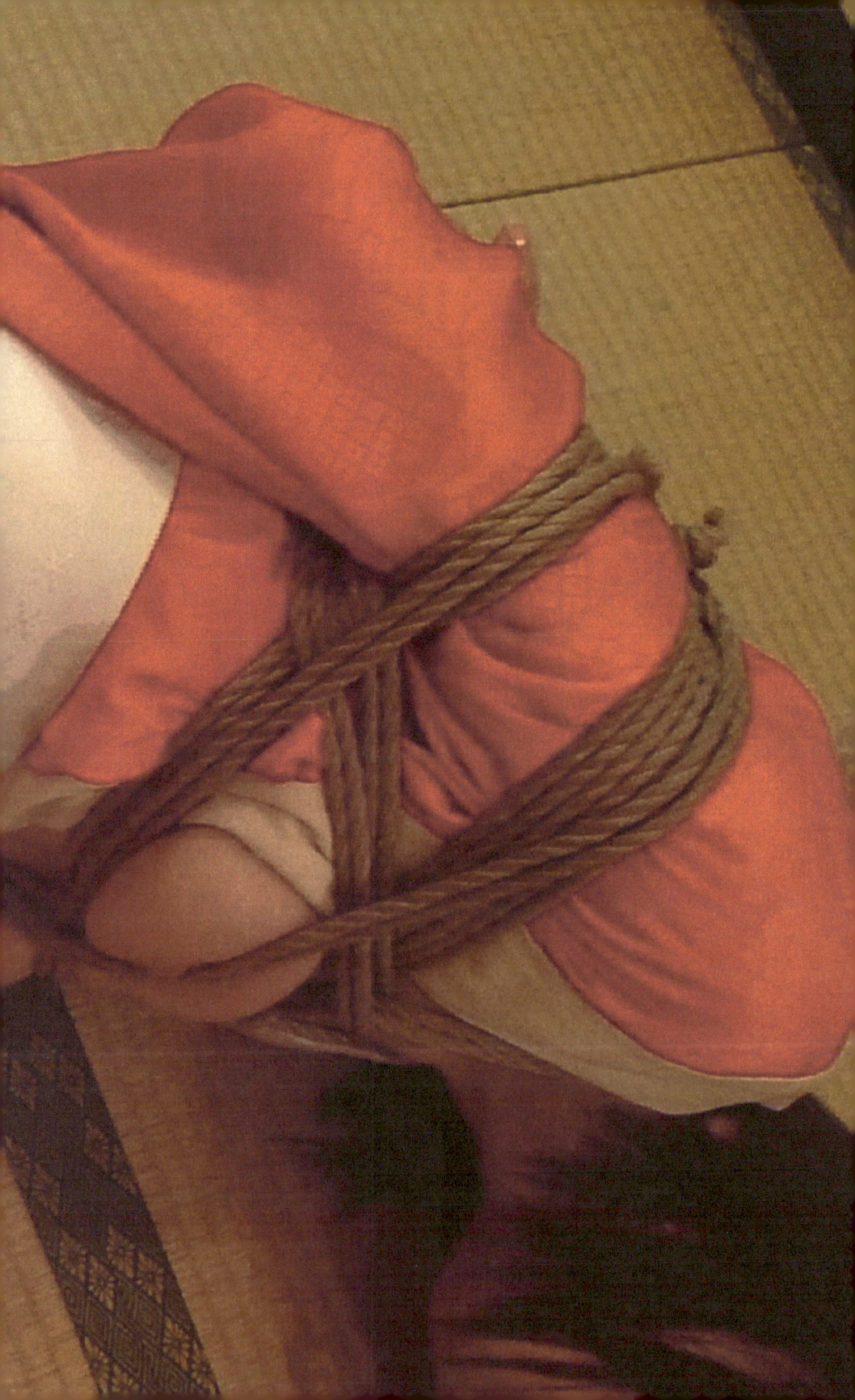

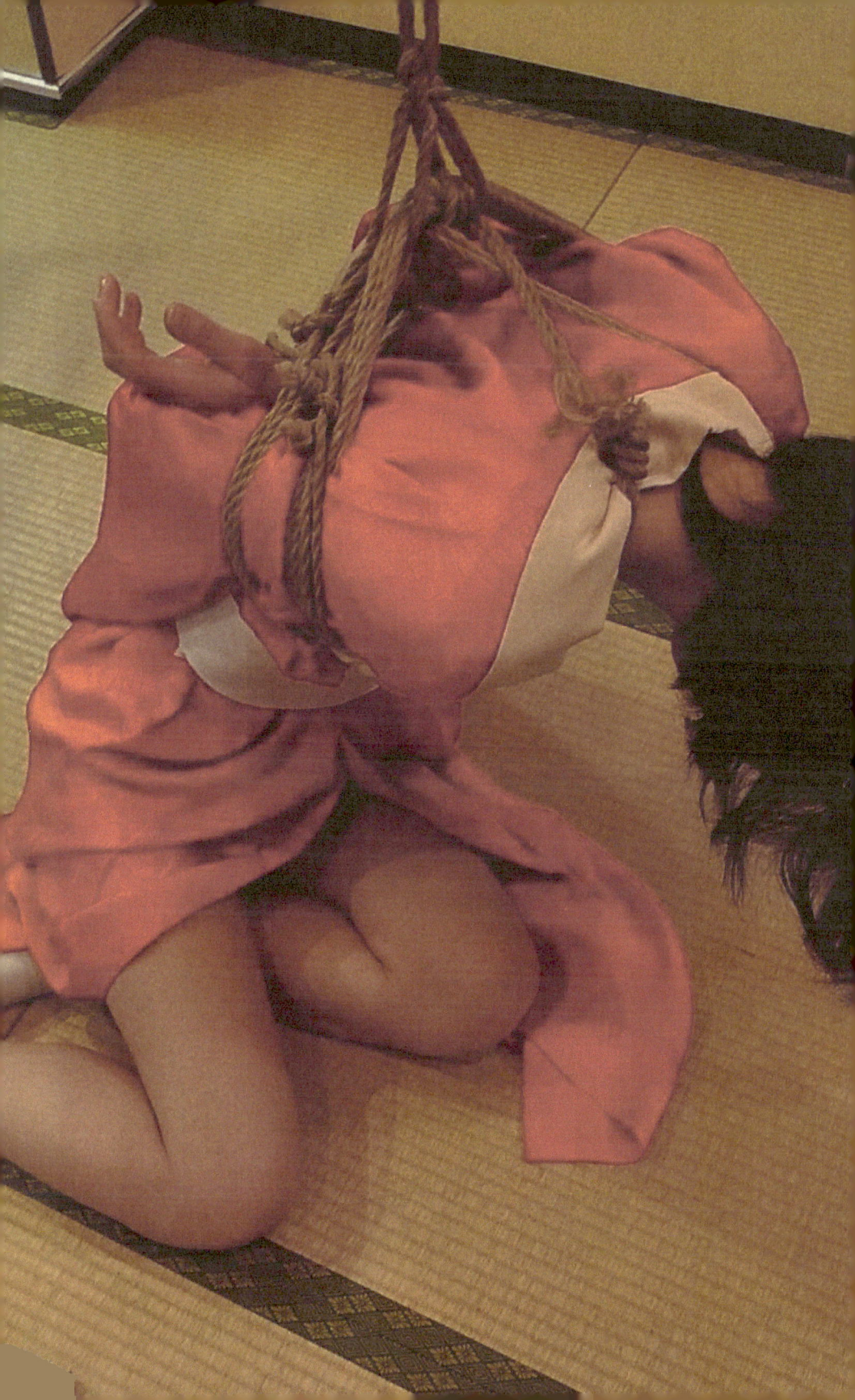

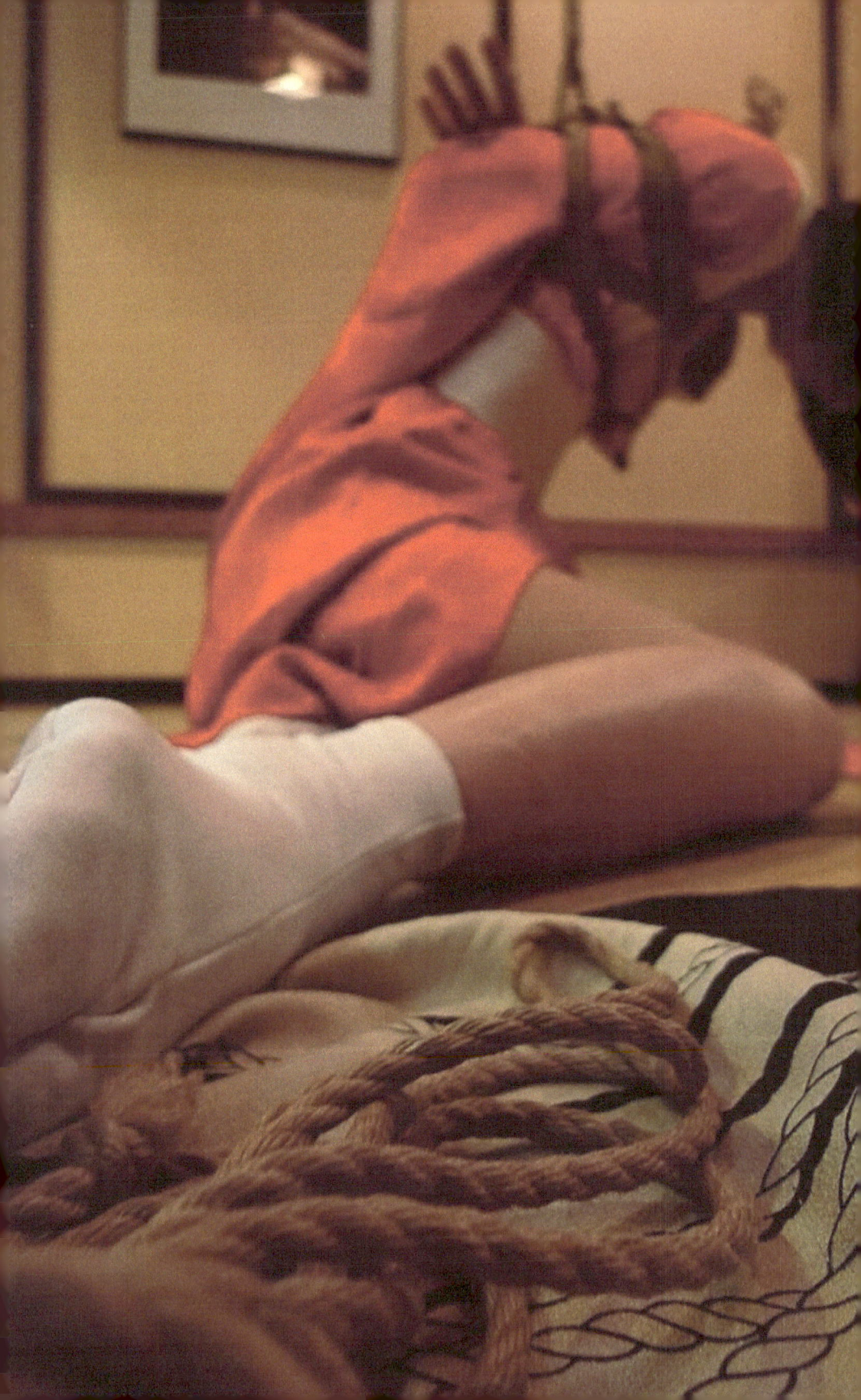

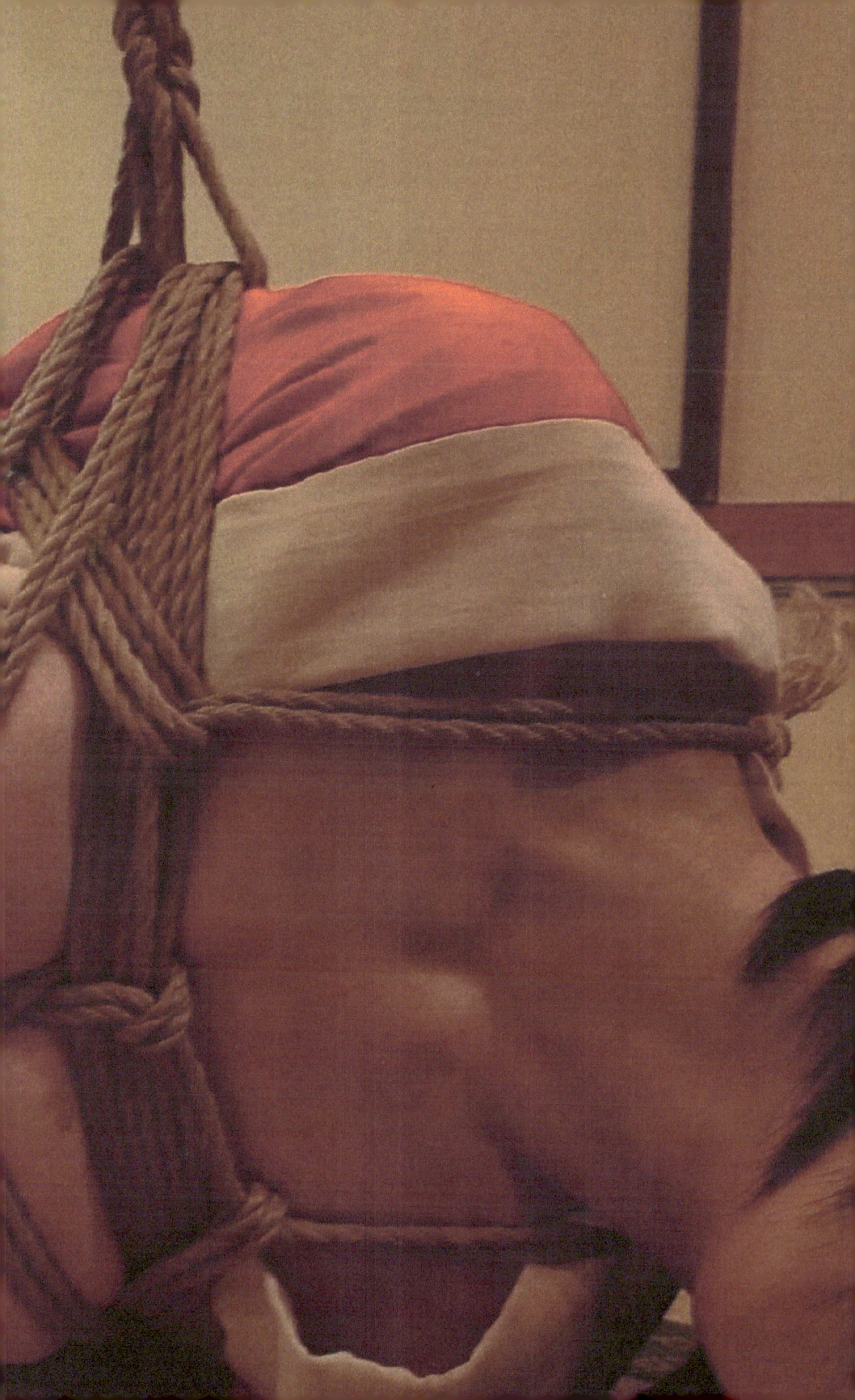

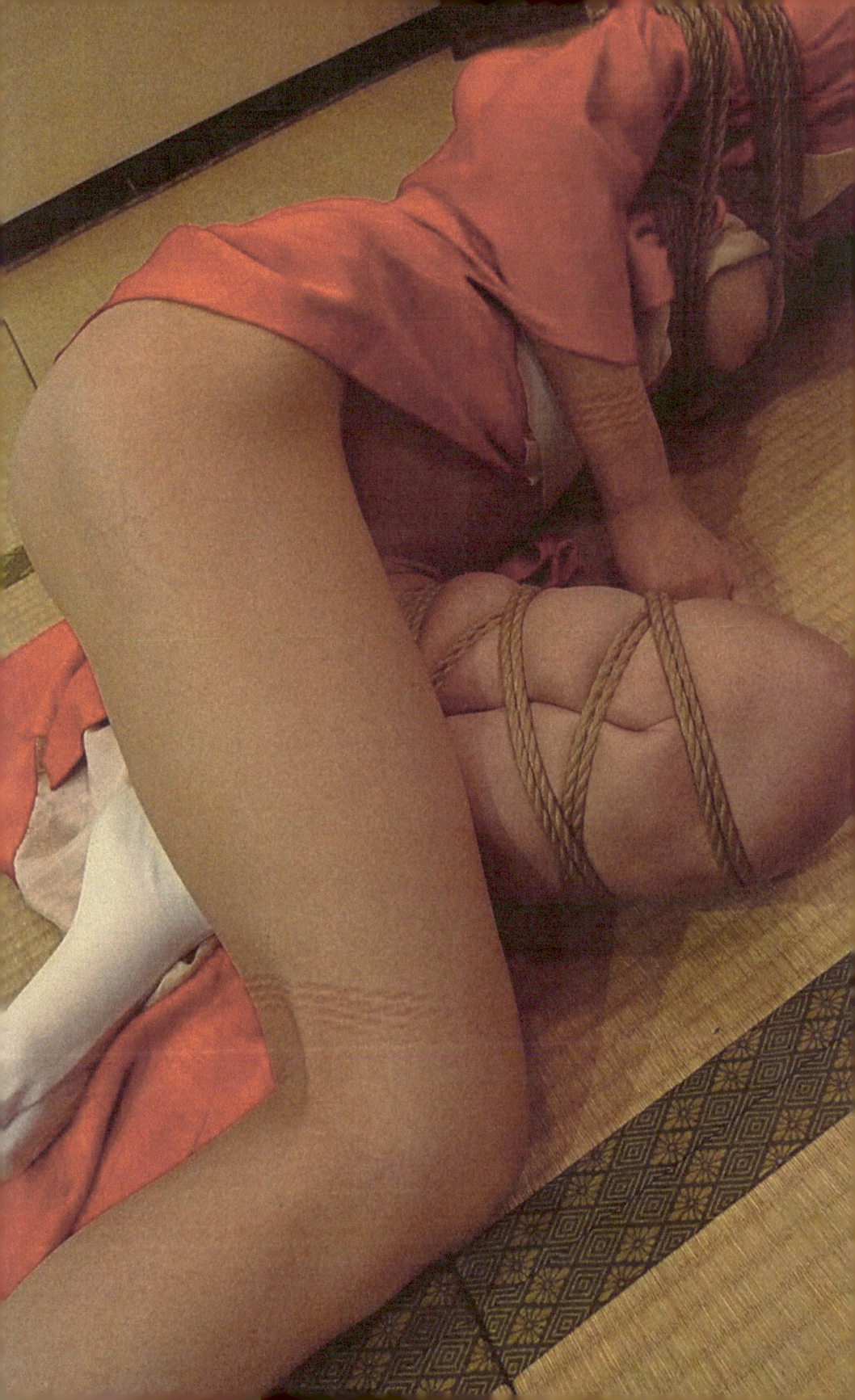

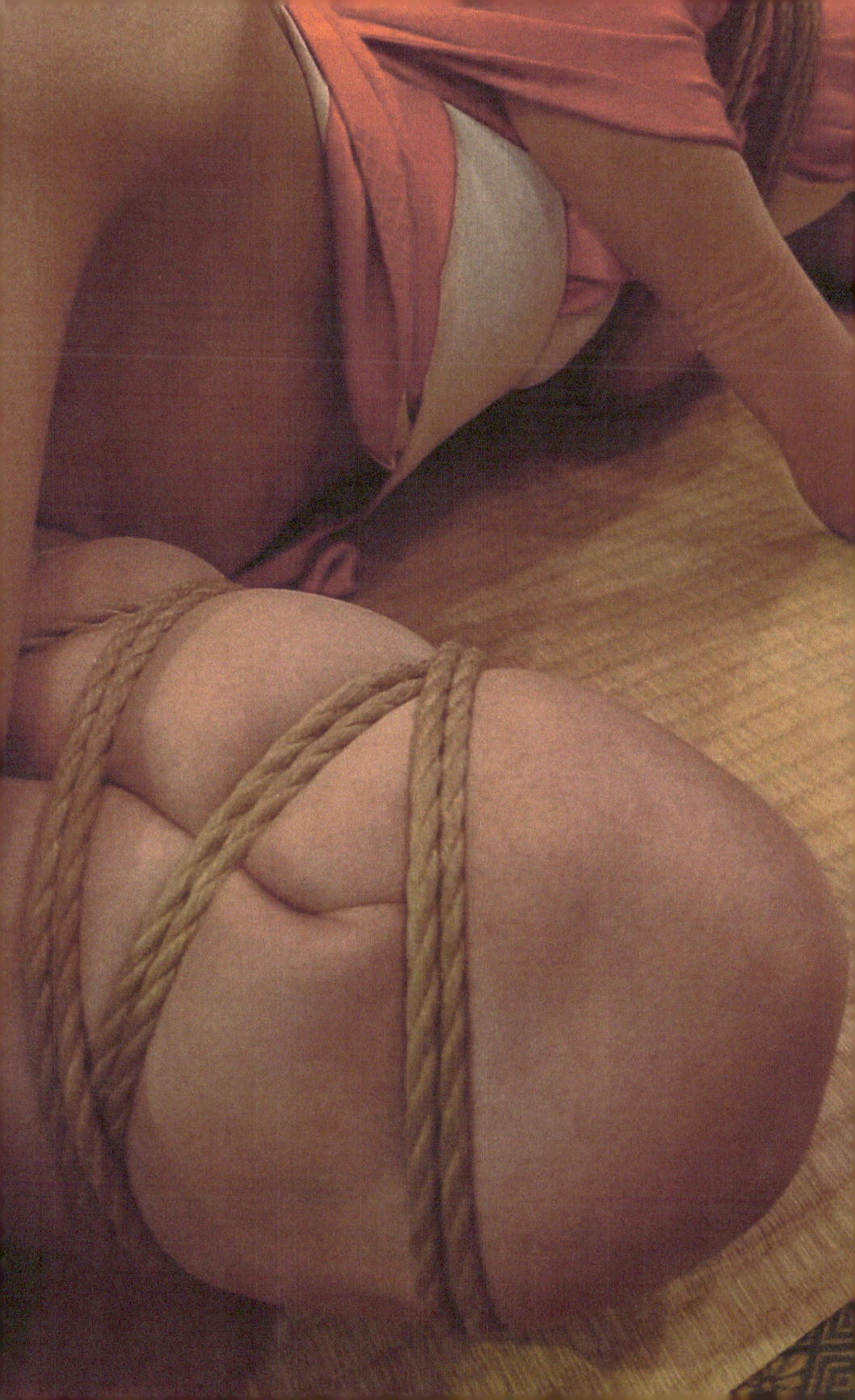

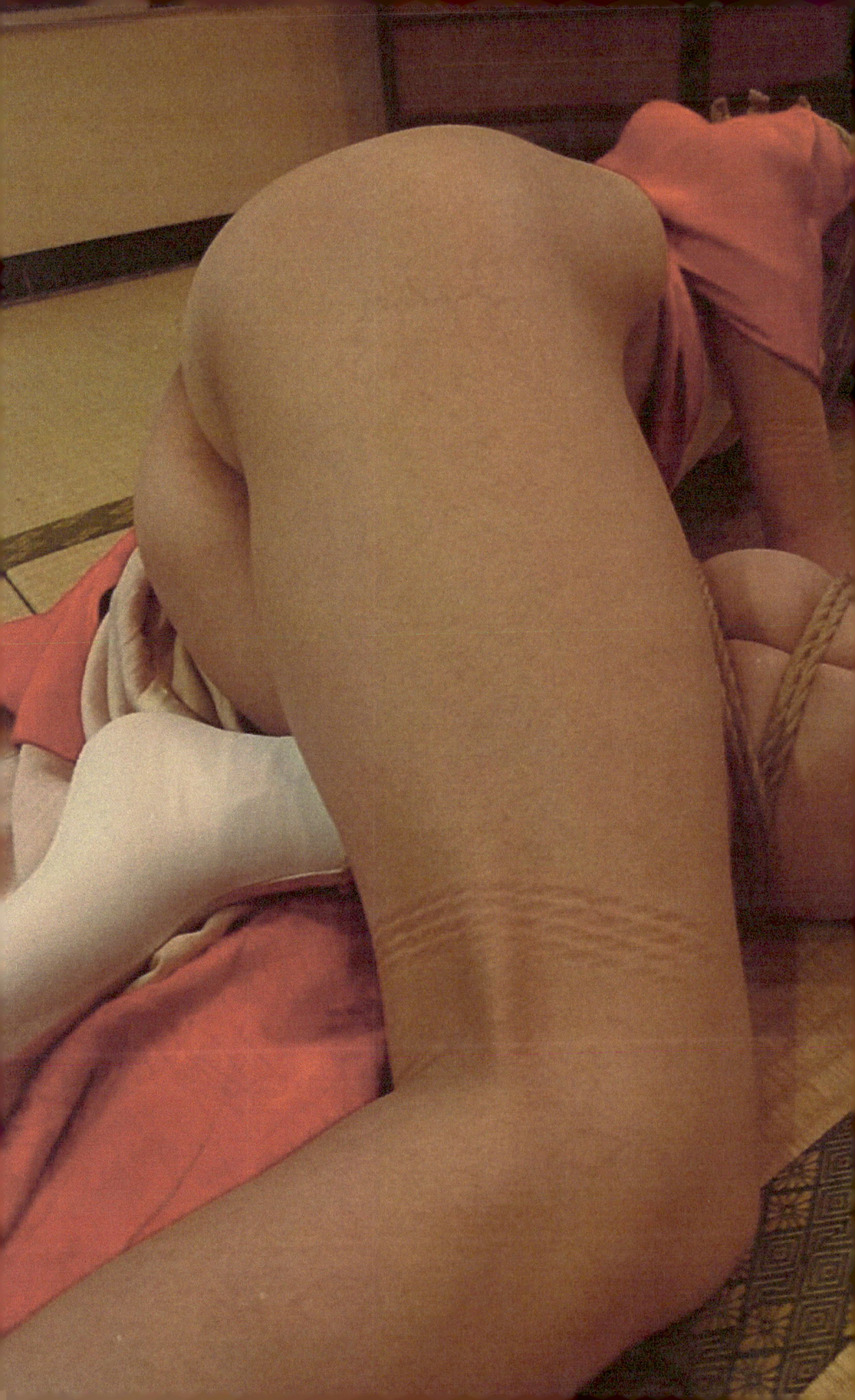

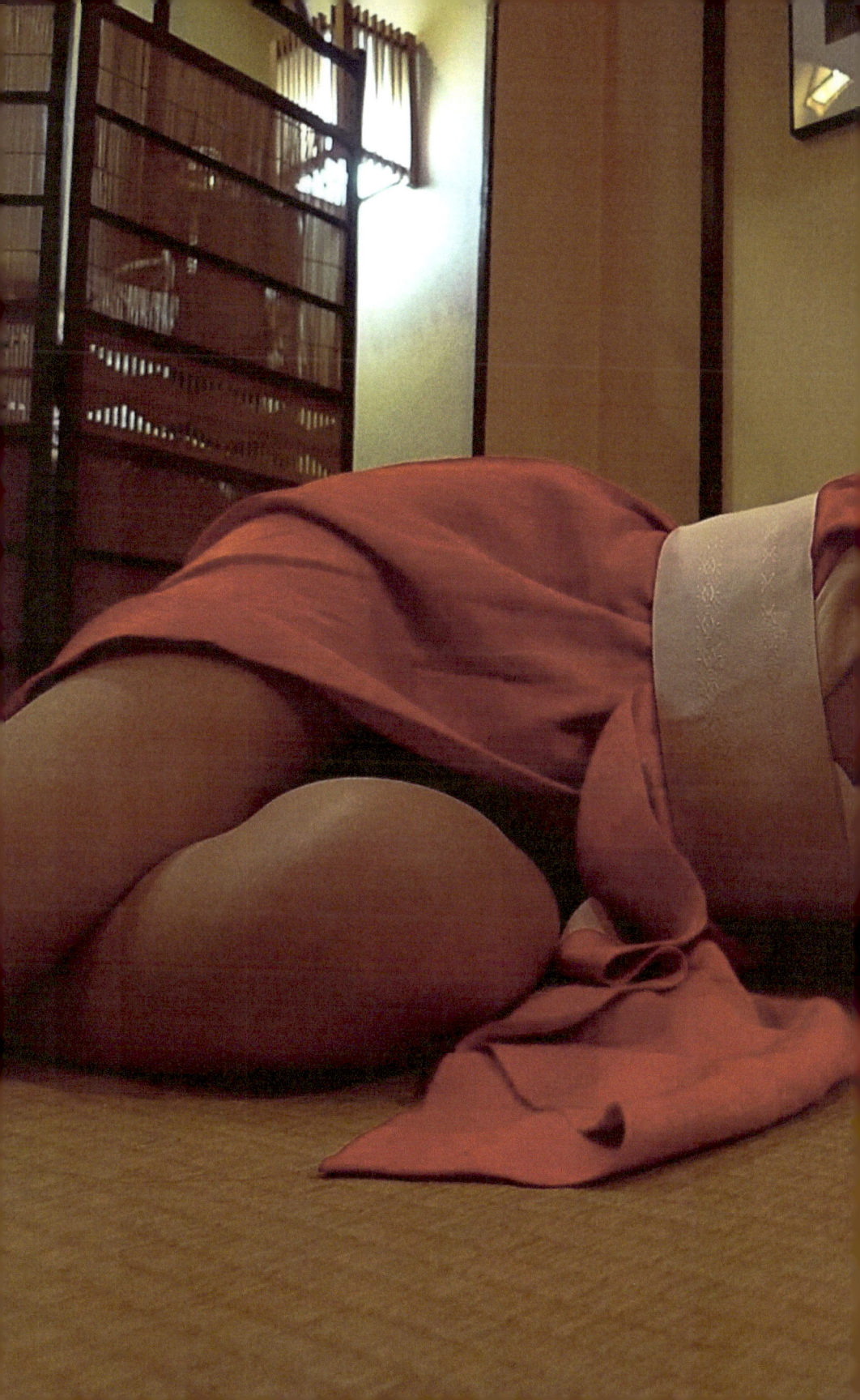

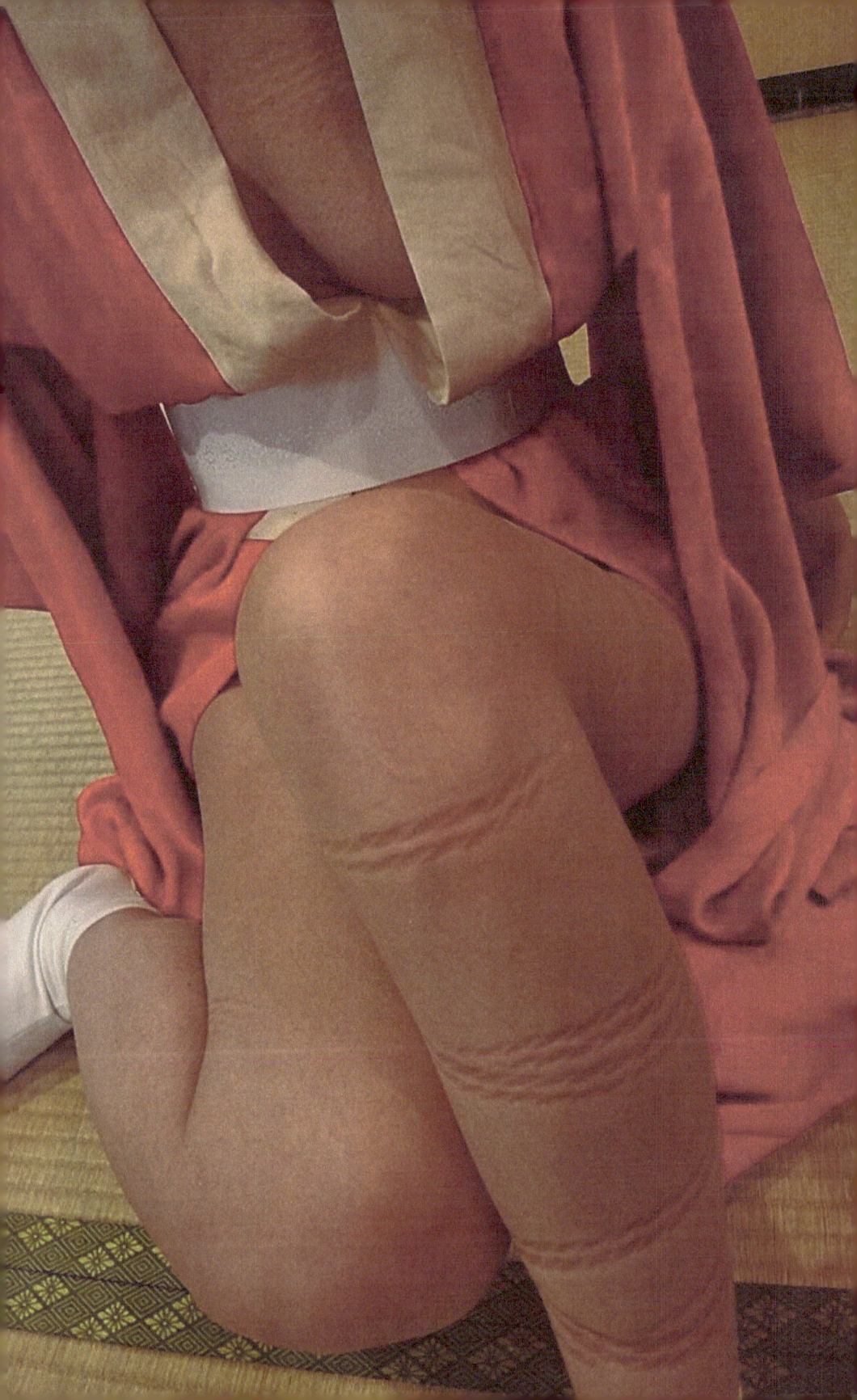

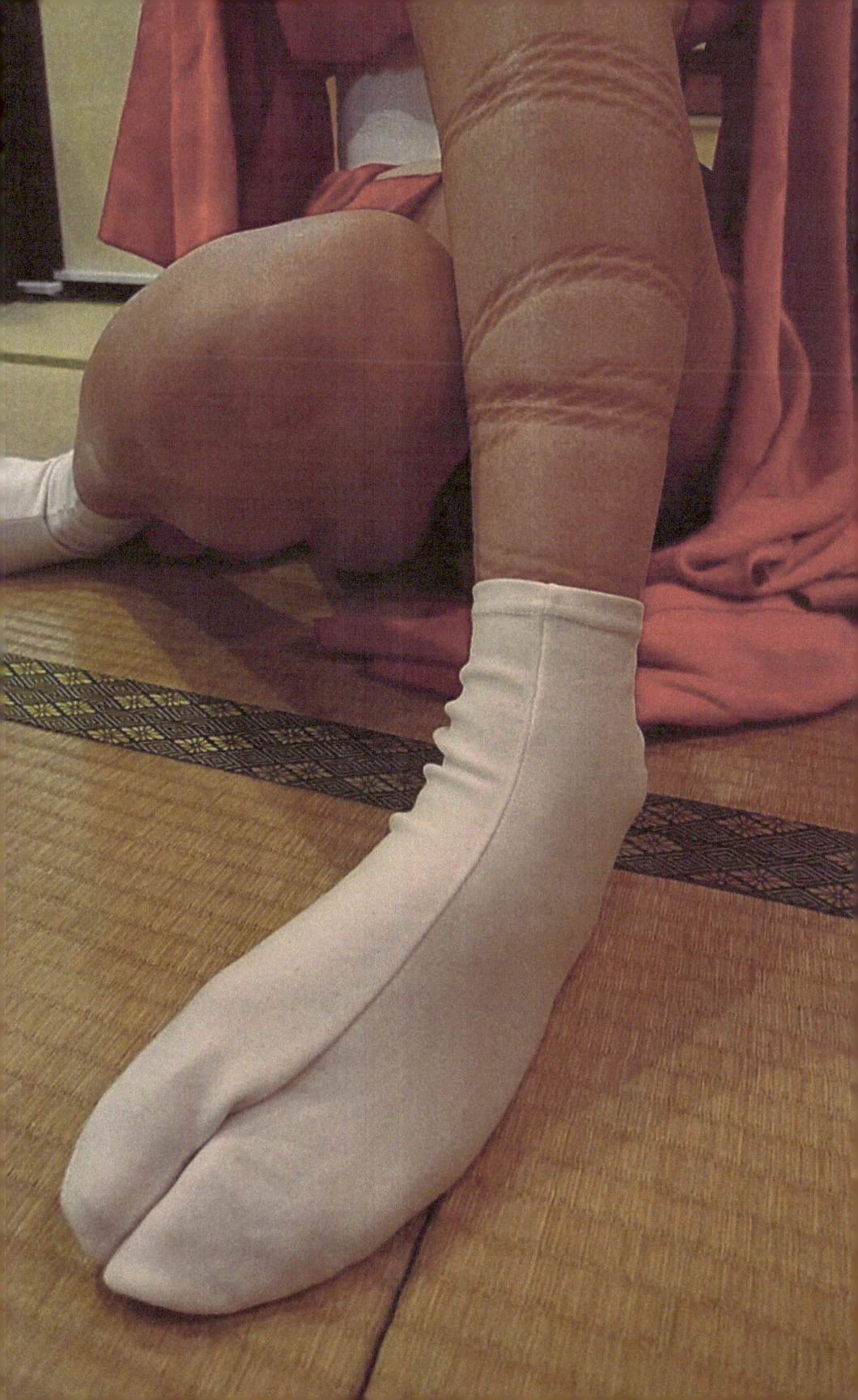

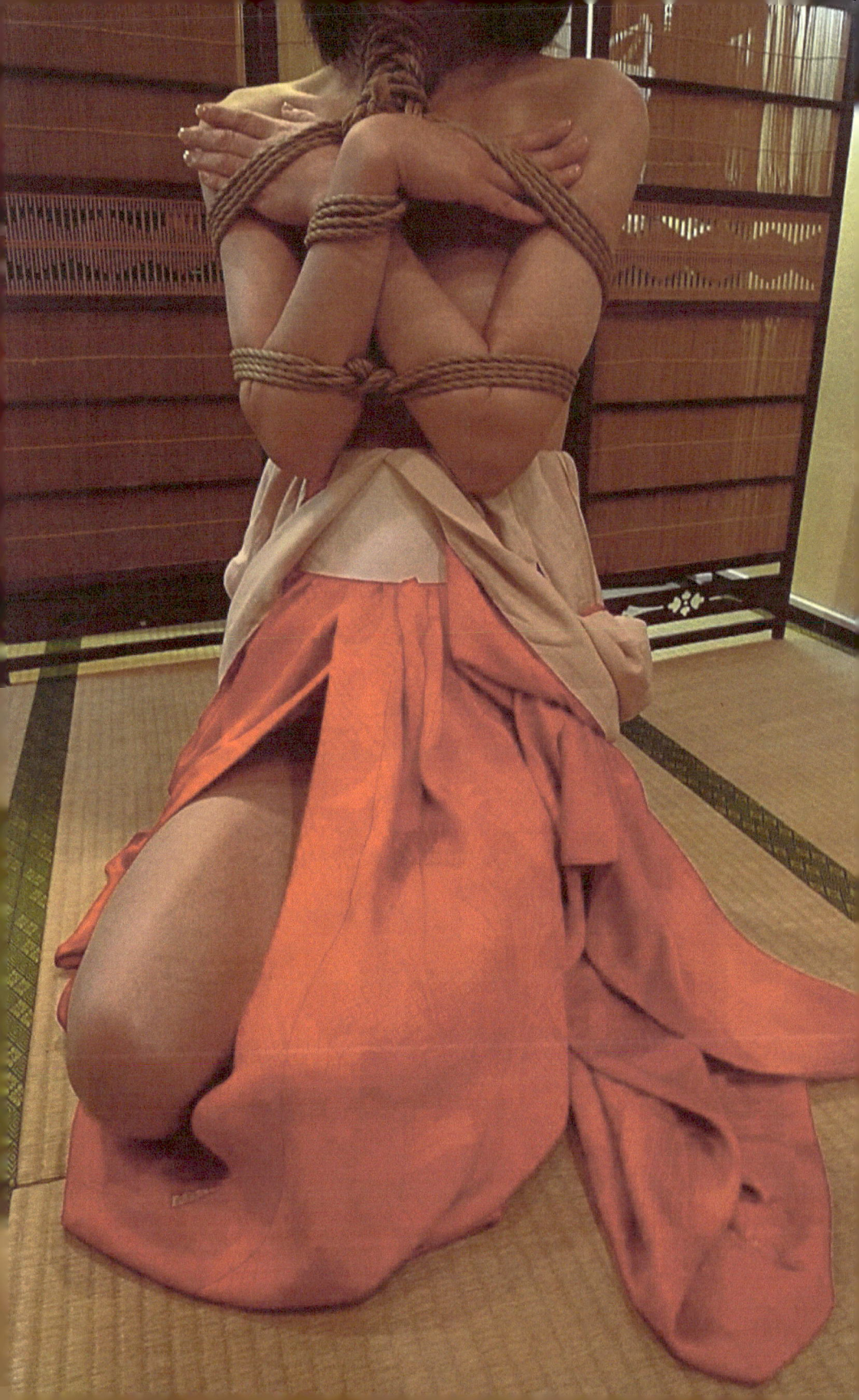

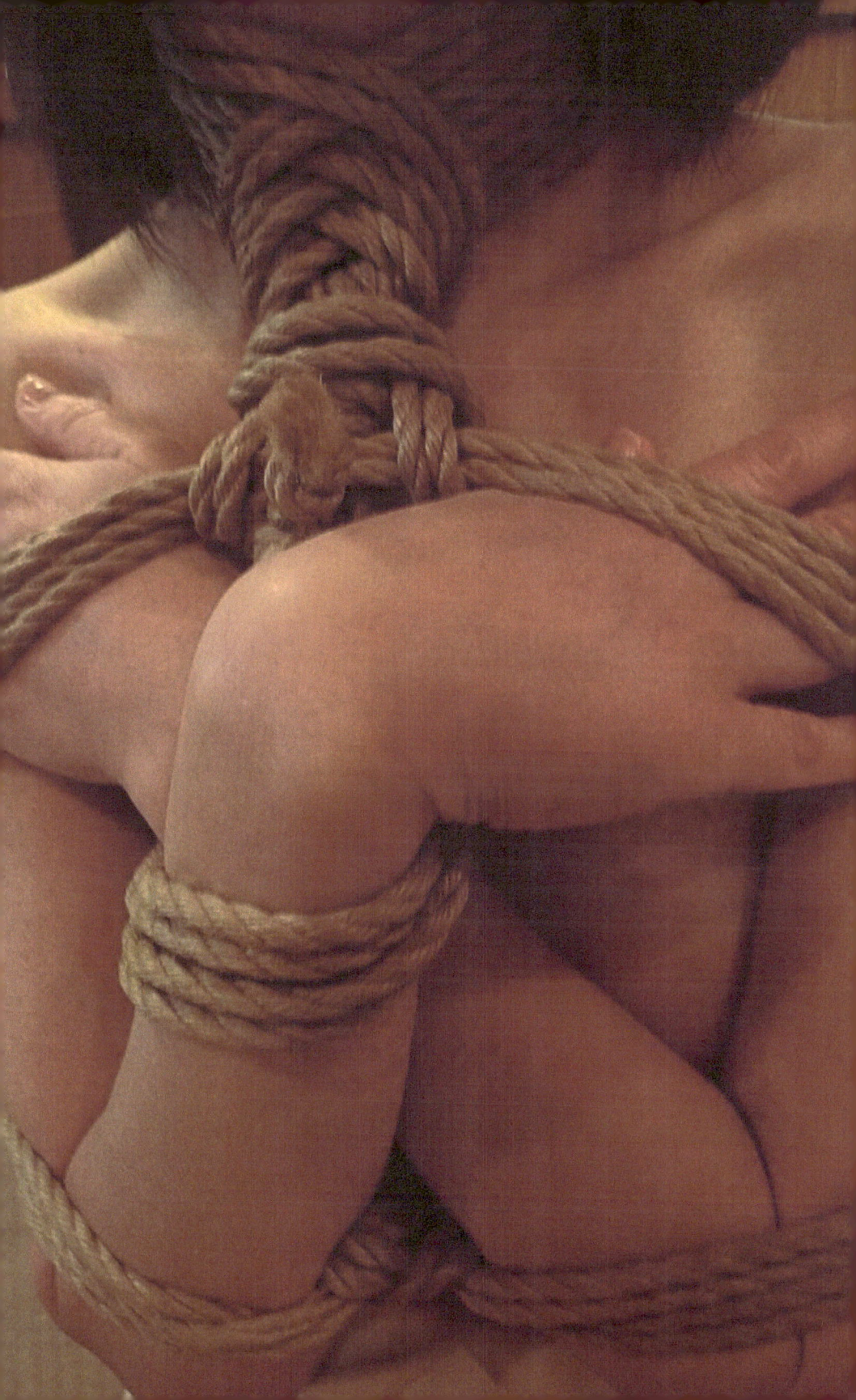

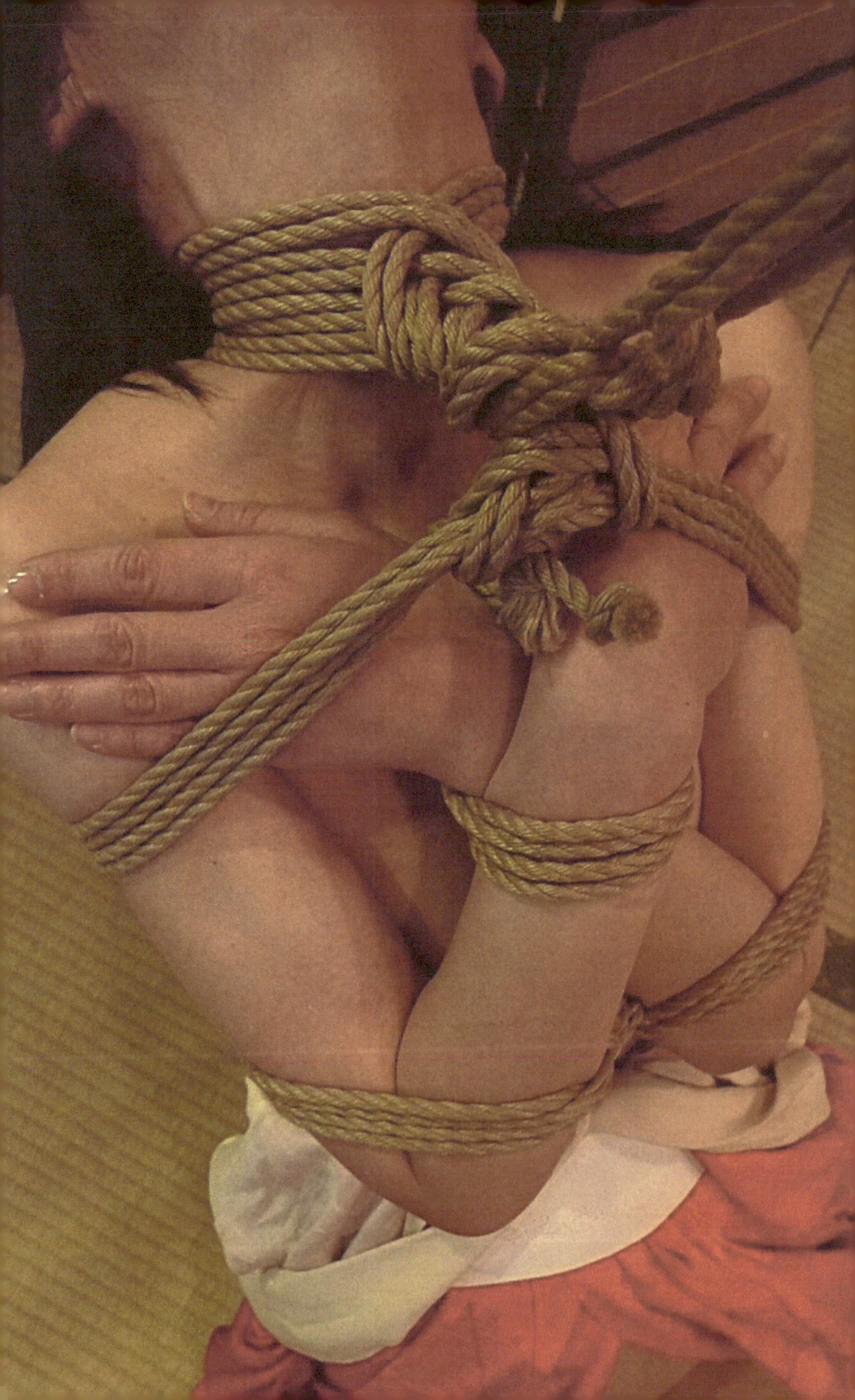

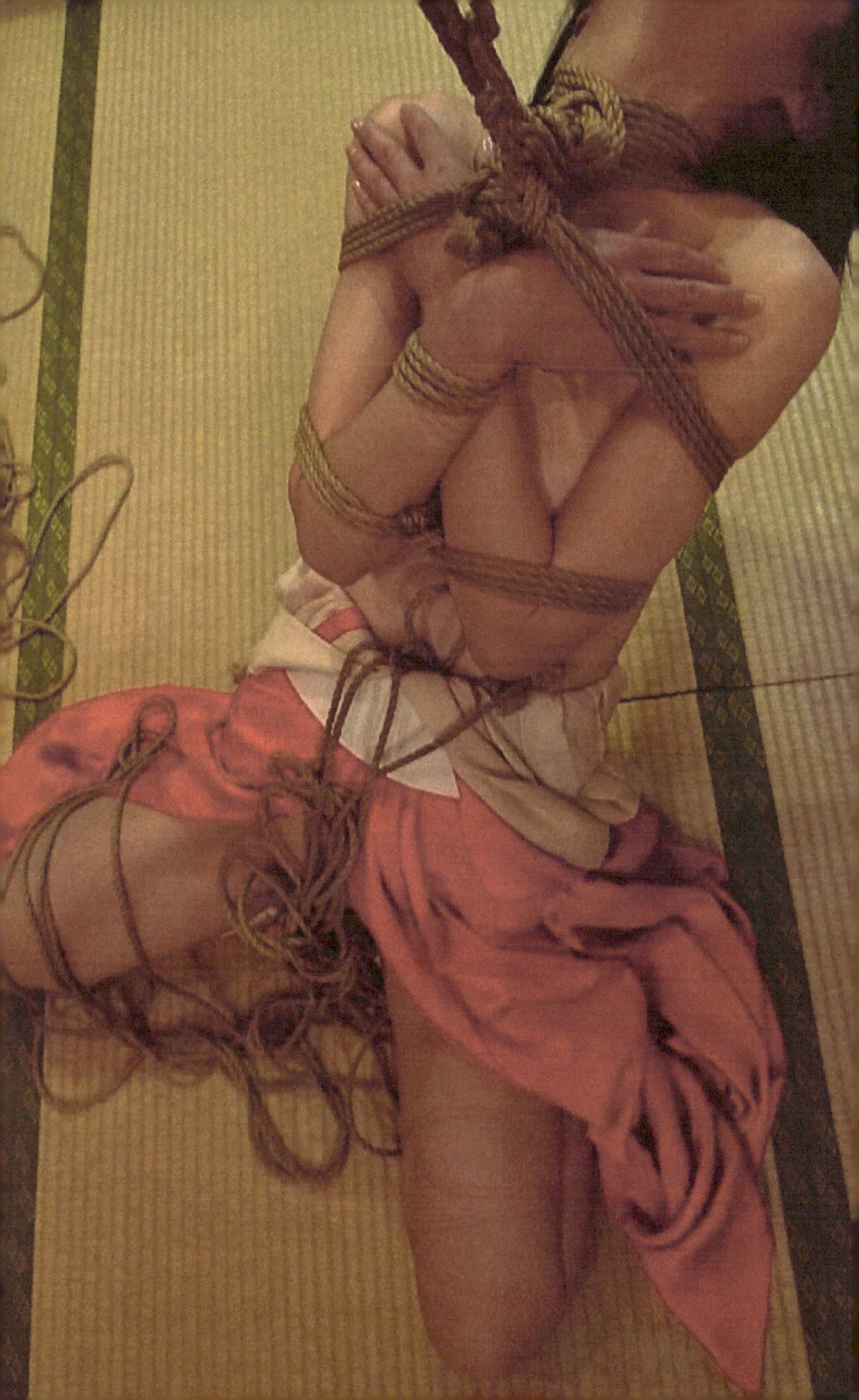

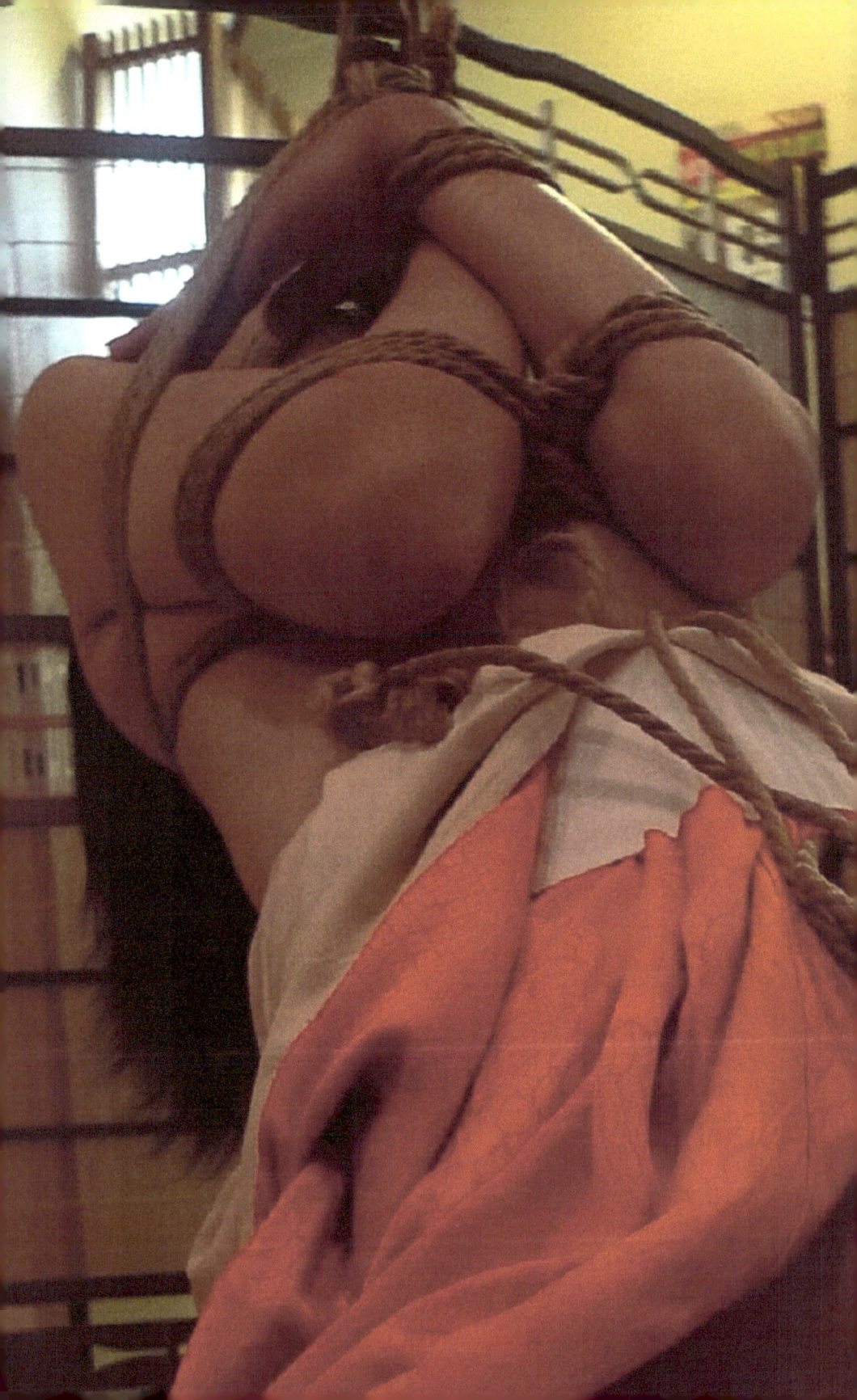

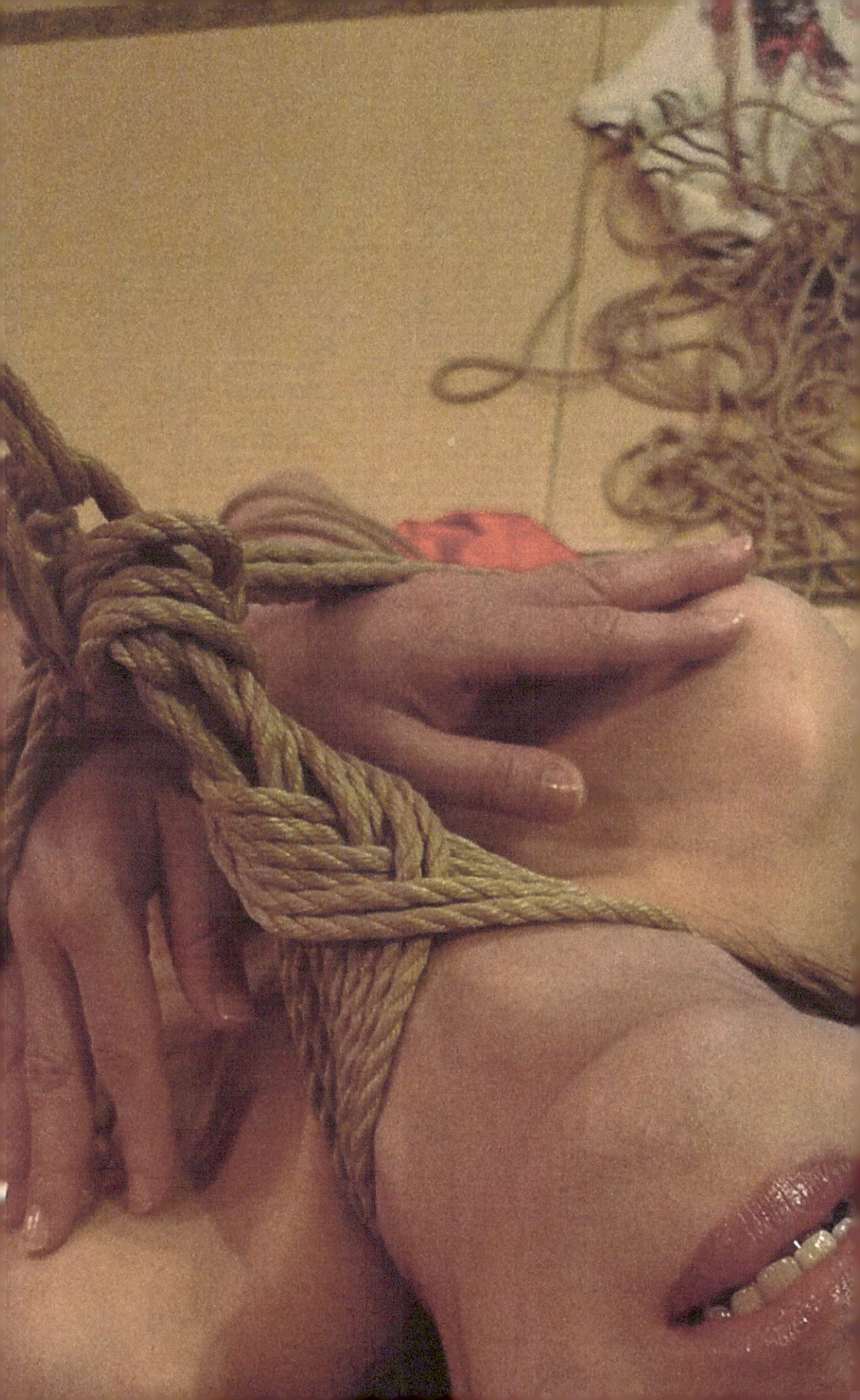

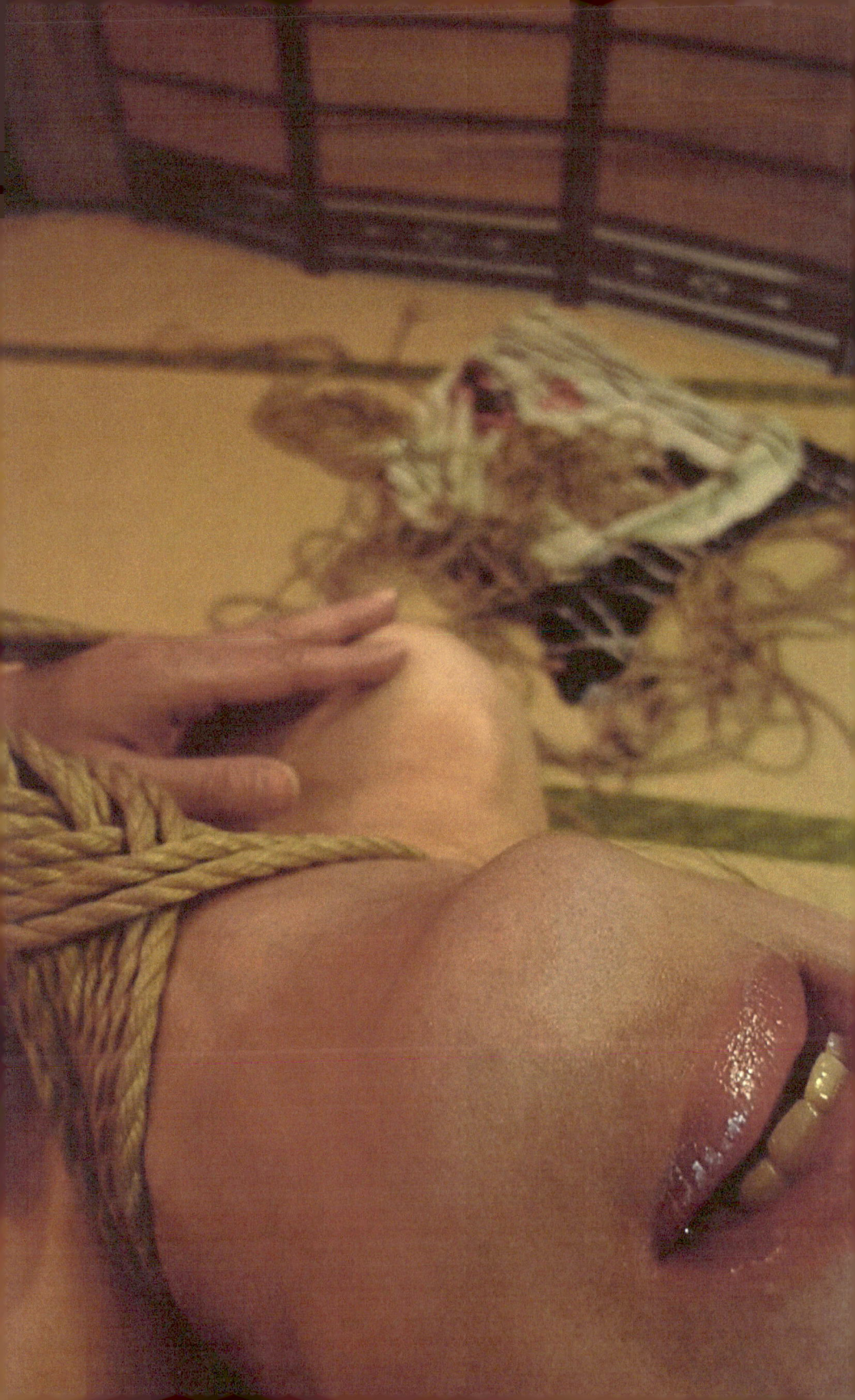

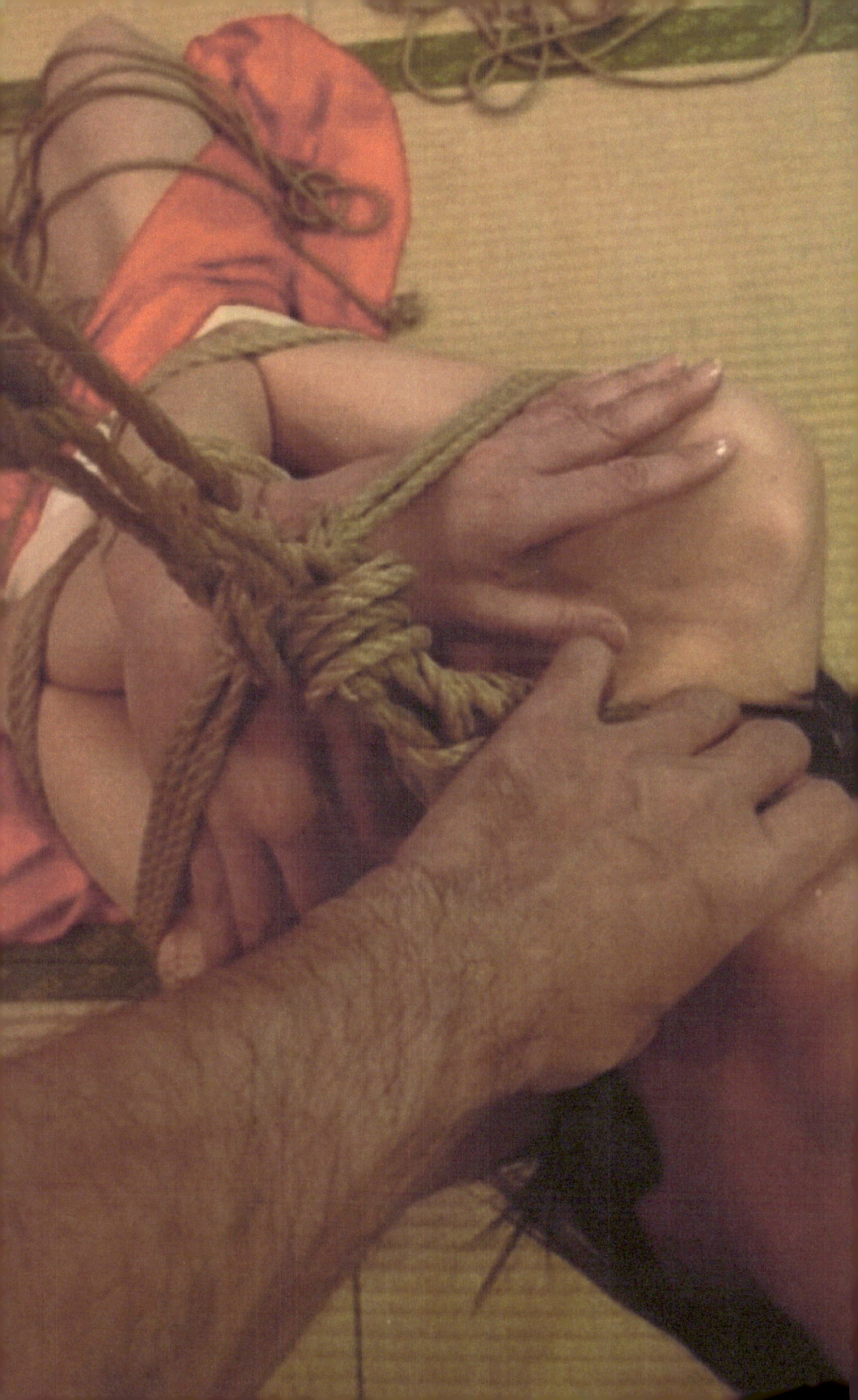

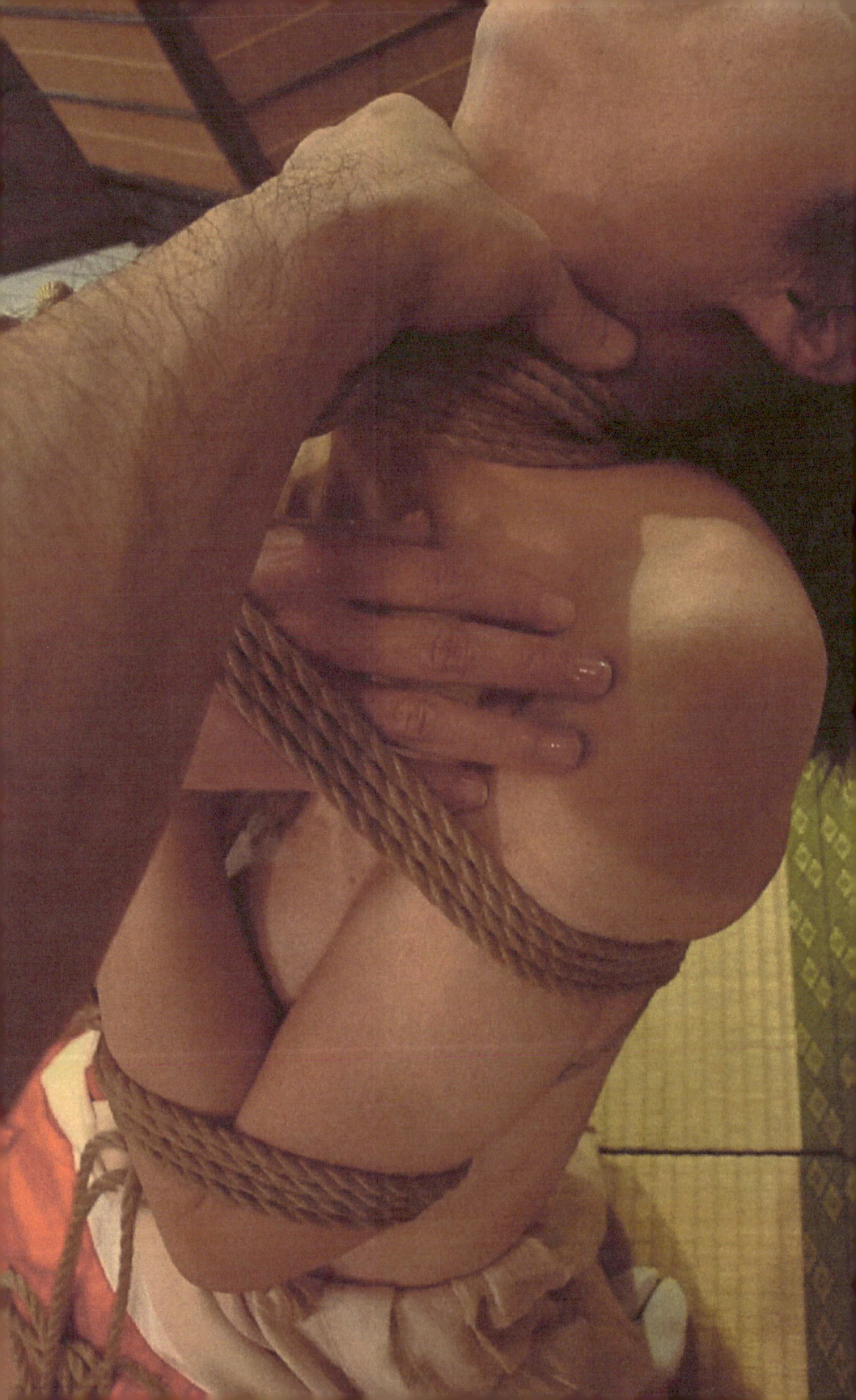

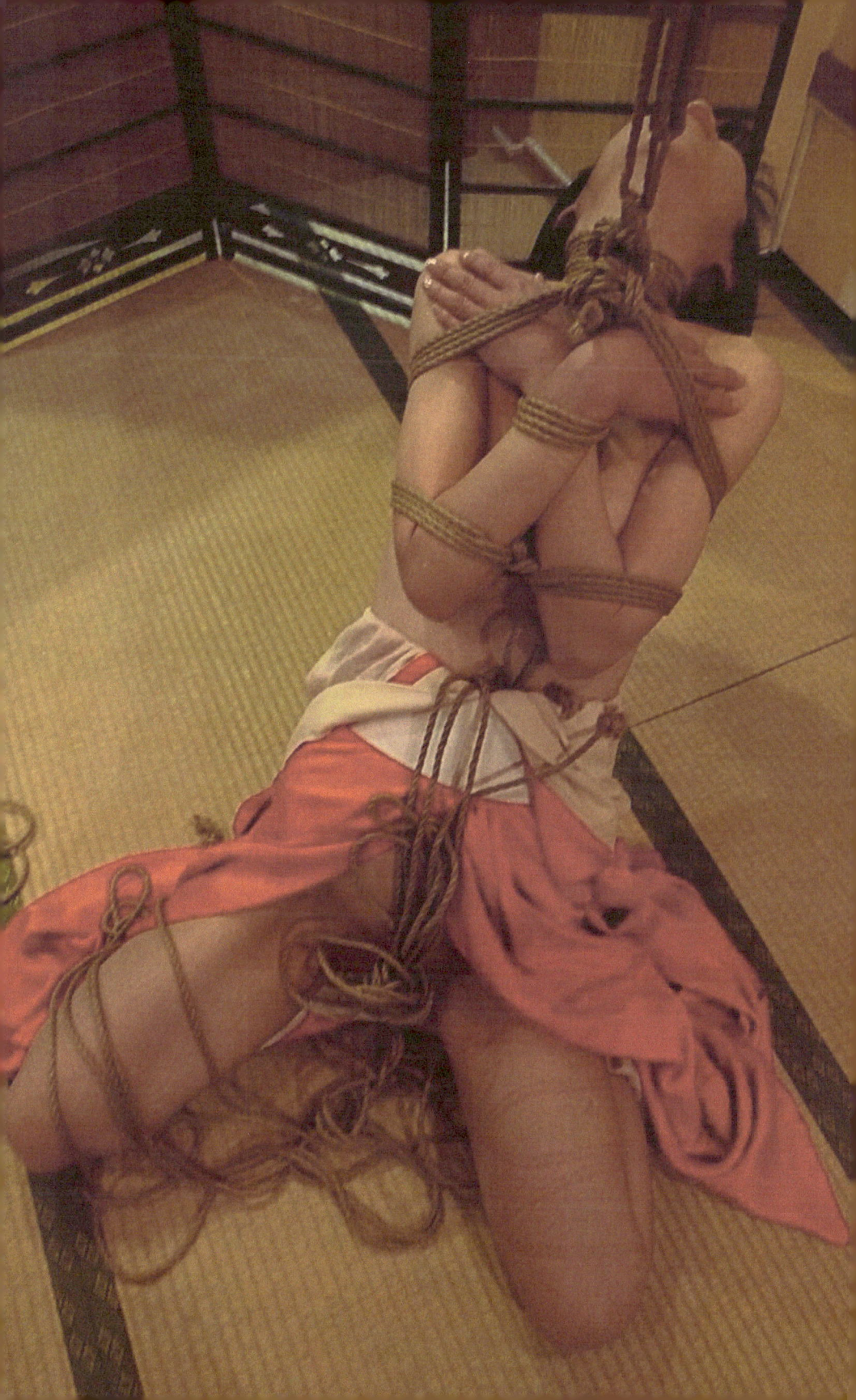

KINBAKU photo book 緊縛写真集

Restraint 拘束

Model:
Yuki Sakurai 櫻井ゆき
http://bit.ly/yuki_sakurai

Kinbakushi:
Shigonawa Bingo 紫護縄びんご
http://shigonawabingo.tumblr.com/

Location:
UBU 初心 http://www.bar-ubu.com/

Published by Sakura Publishing
http://sakurasm.com/English/